I'm the Chef!

Crabtree Publishing Company

.PMB 16A, 350 Fifth Avenue,
Suite 3308, New York,
NY 10118

612 Welland Avenue,
St. Catharines, Ontario
Canada L2M 5V6

Created by **McRae Books**

Coordinating Editor: Ellen Rodger
Project Editor: Lisa Gurusinghe
Production Coordinator: Rosie Gowsell
Production Assistance: Mary-Anne Luzba
Consulting Chef: Dan Fudge

McRae Books Srl.
Project Manager: Anne McRae
Texts: Rosalba Gioffrè
Editor: Alison Wilson
Photography: Marco Lanza, Walter Mericchi
Set Design: Rosalba Gioffrè
Design: Marco Nardi
Layout and cutouts: Ornella Fassio, Adriano Nardi, Giovanni Mattioli
Special thanks to: Mastrociliegia (Fiesole), and Dino Bartolini (Florence), who kindly lent props for photography.
Color separations: Fotolito Toscana, Florence, Italy

CATALOGING-IN-PUBLICATION DATA

Gioffre, Rosalba.
 The Young Chef's Italian cookbook / Rosalba Gioffre [sic.].
 p. cm. -- (I'm the chef)
 Includes index.
 ISBN 0-7787-0279-0 (RLB) -- ISBN 0-7787-0293-6 (pbk.)
 1. Cookery, Italian--Juvenile literature. 2. Quick and easy
cookery--Juvenile literature. [1. Cookery, Italian.]   I. Title. II.
Series.
 TX723 .G478 2001
 641.5945--dc21

00-065996
LC

123456789 Printed and bound in Italy   - Nuova GEP   987654321

I'm the Chef!

The Young Chef's
ITALIAN
COOKBOOK

🌳 **Crabtree**
www.crabtreebooks.com

Contents

DISCLAIMER

The recipes in this book are suitable for children aged nine and up. They have all been prepared in our test kitchen by a mother of three young children and are safe for children of that age. Throughout the book, we have included tips for safety in the kitchen. However, since cooking involves the use of knives, boiling water, and other potentially dangerous equipment and procedures, it is strongly recommended that an adult supervises children at all times while they are preparing the recipes in this book. The publishers and copyright owners will not accept any responsibility for accidents that may occur when children are preparing these dishes.

Introduction

Italian food is not only delicious, it is also easy to prepare. This makes it especially suitable for young chefs. In this book, there are fifteen popular recipes with step-by-step photographs. By following the instructions carefully you can surprise your friends and family with some delicious food. Each recipe also has special tips and tricks to help a young chef get it right from the start. The central pages (22–23) focus on *Carnevale,* showing the fun, and the food, that Italian children enjoy at that time of year. So, have fun, or as they say in Italy, *Buon divertimento!*

Bruschetta

Toast with tomato and basil topping

This delicious summertime snack is served all over Italy, but it is especially popular in the south where tomatoes are plentiful. The name of this dish is pronounced "brusketta," because in Italian the letters "ch" have a hard sound, as in the English word "architect."

Ingredients

2 thick slices heavy white bakery bread

2 cloves garlic, peeled

6 fresh basil leaves

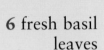

2 tablespoons (30 ml) extra-virgin olive oil

salt and ground black pepper to taste

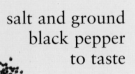

2 large ripe salad tomatoes

Rinse your fingertips in a little vinegar to eliminate the strong smell of garlic.

1 Toast two slices of bread until light golden brown. Rub each slice with a clove of garlic. The crispy surface of the toast will "grate" the garlic and quickly absorb it.

Utensils

CUTTING BOARD

BREAD KNIFE

2 Rinse the tomatoes and wipe them dry with paper towels. **Chop** the tomatoes into cubes and spread them over the toast. Take special care with the knife. You do not need a very sharp one. An ordinary bread knife is fine.

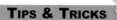
TIPS & TRICKS

Bruschetta *makes a healthy after school snack. Quantities given here will be enough for one or two. For better flavor, let the tomato mixture sit for at least one hour. Spread the mixture on the bread just before serving so that the toast does not become soggy. Ask an adult to help when working with knives.*

3 Rinse the basil and shake lightly until dry. Use your fingertips to tear the basil into pieces and **sprinkle** it over the tomatoes. Season with a little salt.

4 **Drizzle** the *bruschetta* with olive oil to taste. If you like spicy food, sprinkle a little black pepper over the top.

Crostini

Chicken liver toasts

Don't be put off by some of the ingredients in this recipe. The chicken livers and **anchovies** mix in with the other ingredients to make a delicious topping for the toast. This dish is found all over Italy, but originally comes from Tuscany, where it is served as an *antipasto* or **appetizer** along with a platter of ham and salami.

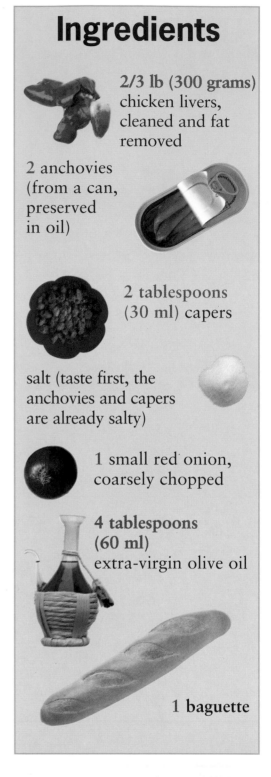

Ingredients

2/3 lb (300 grams) chicken livers, cleaned and fat removed

2 anchovies (from a can, preserved in oil)

2 tablespoons (30 ml) capers

salt (taste first, the anchovies and capers are already salty)

1 small red onion, coarsely chopped

4 tablespoons (60 ml) extra-virgin olive oil

1 baguette

TIPS & TRICKS

You will need a sharp knife to chop the chicken livers and onion. Be very careful while doing this. Hold the knife well up the handle and keep your fingers away from the blade. Ask an adult to help. Junior cooks in Italy use a half-moon chopper because they are much safer.

1 Use a bread knife with a **serrated** blade to slice the bread into rounds about ½ inch (1 cm) thick and toast lightly.

Utensils

HALF-MOON CHOPPER

CUTTING BOARD

FOOD MILL

SKILLET (FRYING PAN)

2 Rinse the chicken livers and **chop coarsely**. Cook in a **skillet** over high heat for 1 minute. Then add the oil, onion, anchovies, and capers. Cook for 3–4 minutes. With an adult's help, pour in ½ cup (125 ml) hot water, and cook for 8–10 more minutes.

3 Taste the mixture to see if it needs salt. Remove the skillet from the heat and put the mixture into a food processor with 2 tablespoons (30 ml) of warm water. Blend until creamy.

4 Spread the mixture on the toasted bread. Arrange on a dish and serve.

Pizza

Margherita pizza

Even if you have a great pizza place in your neighborhood, try making your own at home. Making pizza is simple and fun. Two main things to remember are **kneading** the dough properly and leaving it long enough to rise. This recipe is for the classic Margherita pizza, which was invented in Naples for Queen Margherita of Savoy, in June 1889. You can vary it by adding ham or mushrooms, or some of your other favorite toppings.

1 In a bowl, **dissolve** the yeast in ½ cup (125 ml) of warm water, mixing well. Set the yeast aside for 15 minutes. **Sift** the flour and salt into another large bowl.

2 Gradually work the yeast mixture into the flour. Flour your hands and use your knuckles and fists to work the dough until it is smooth and elastic.

3 Form the dough into a ball, and wrap it loosely in a clean cotton cloth. Leave it in the bowl in a warm sheltered place to rise or cover the bowl with a cloth for at least 30 minutes. Preheat the oven to 450°F (230°C).

4 Oil a rectangular or circular pizza pan and use your fingertips to gently stretch the dough out to cover the bottom.

5 Open the can of crushed tomatoes and spread them over the dough. If using whole tomatoes, put them in a bowl and squish them with your fingers first. Shred or **grate** the mozzarella cheese and spread it on top of the tomatoes.

6 Sprinkle with the salt and oregano. Drizzle with the oil and bake in the oven for about 20 minutes.

Ingredients

3¼ cups (800 ml) all-purpose (plain) flour

1 teaspoon (5 ml) salt

1 cake (⅔ oz/ 20 g) compressed baker's yeast or **1 package** active dry yeast

1 can (13 oz/400 ml) crushed tomatoes

¾ cup (5 oz/150 g) mozzarella cheese

1 tablespoon (15 ml) extra-virgin olive oil

dash of fresh or dried oregano and basil

13

Utensils

LARGE MIXING BOWL

PIZZA TRAY

TIPS & TRICKS

Ask an adult to open the can of tomatoes and also to take the pizza out of the oven. If you do handle the hot pizza tray yourself, be sure to use thick oven mitts to protect your hands.

Penne al pomodoro

Pasta with tomato and basil sauce

Pasta is the national dish in Italy, where it is served every day. Tomato sauce is one of the most popular toppings for pasta. Tomatoes were introduced to Italy from Mexico and Central America by Spanish explorers during the 16th century. Serve the dish with style by saying *"Buon appetito!,"* which means "Enjoy!"

Ingredients

1 can (13 oz/ 400 ml) tomatoes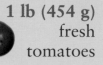

OR

1 lb (454 g) fresh tomatoes

6 fresh basil leaves, torn into pieces

2 cloves garlic, peeled (chopped or whole)

1 lb (454 g) penne pasta

4 tablespoons (60 ml) olive oil

4 tablespoons (60 ml) grated Parmesan cheese

dash of table salt for the sauce and **2 tablespoons (30 ml)** coarse salt to cook the pasta

If you have some extra sauce left over, spoon it over a slice of toasted bread for a tasty snack.

1 Fill a big pot half way with cold water and place on the stove over high heat. Drain the liquid from the canned tomatoes, place them in a pan, and mash with a fork. If fresh tomatoes are used, peel them with a potato peeler or knife, chop them into cubes, and place in a pan.

15

2 Add the olive oil, garlic, and salt to the tomatoes. Place the pan over medium heat and partially cover. Cook for about 30 minutes, stirring often to prevent sticking. With an adult's help remove from the heat and add the basil.

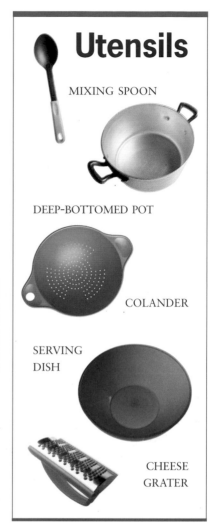

Utensils

MIXING SPOON

DEEP-BOTTOMED POT

COLANDER

SERVING DISH

CHEESE GRATER

3 When the water in the pot is boiling, add the salt and then the penne. Cook for the amount of time shown on the package, stirring often. Drain the pasta in the colander and transfer it to a serving dish.

4 Spoon the tomato sauce over the cooked pasta and mix well. **Grate** the parmesan cheese over the penne. If the cheese is already grated, sprinkle over the pasta. Serve immediately.

This sauce is good with all pasta shapes, including spaghetti, macaroni, and rotini. Be sure to try it with wholewheat or spinach pasta too!

TIPS & TRICKS

Be very careful when draining the pasta. The large pot of boiling water and pasta will be very heavy. Ask an adult to help you lift it. The trick with pasta is getting the cooking time right. It should be soft but still firm when you chew it. Do not cook it so much that it gets mushy and tasteless!

Tagliatelle
Fresh pasta with tomato sauce

Tagliatelle is a fresh noodle pasta that comes from Emilia-Romagna in central Italy. It should be ⅓ inch (8 mm) wide. If it is wider than this, it is known as *pappadelle* and if it is thinner, it is called *tagliolini*. The sauce recipe is also from Emilia-Romagna. It features delicious Parma ham, called *prosciutto,* which is a specialty from the city of Parma in that region.

Ingredients

1 lb (454 g) fresh *tagliatelle* pasta

5 oz (150 g) *prosciutto* (Parma ham)

4 fresh tomatoes or 1 lb (454 g) canned tomatoes

½ cup (125 ml) butter

dash table salt for the sauce and **2 tablespoons** (30 ml) coarse salt to cook the pasta

6 tablespoons (90 ml) grated Parmesan cheese

1 Place a big pot of cold water on the stove over high heat. Put the *prosciutto* on a cutting board. Cut it first into strips and then into cubes. Hold the knife firmly in one hand and keep your fingers away from the blade.

2 Use a potato peeler or knife to peel the tomatoes, then chop them coarsely, or open a can of tomatoes and squash them in a bowl using a fork. Place the tomatoes in a deep-bottomed saucepan together with the *prosciutto* and the butter.

3 **Mix** well and cook over medium heat for about 30 minutes. Stir occasionally with a wooden spoon. Add salt to taste.

4 While the sauce is cooking, cook the *tagliatelle* in a large pot of boiling water. Add the coarse salt before you add the pasta. Grate the Parmesan cheese.

5 When the pasta is cooked, drain it in a colander. Transfer it to a large serving dish. Ladle the tomato sauce over the top and sprinkle with the Parmesan. **Toss** well and serve hot.

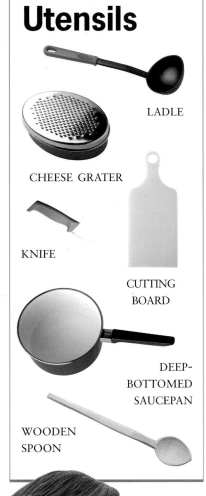

Utensils

LADLE

CHEESE GRATER

KNIFE

CUTTING BOARD

DEEP-BOTTOMED SAUCEPAN

WOODEN SPOON

Pasta al pesto

Pasta with basil sauce

This pasta sauce is quick and easy to make. You just have to mix the ingredients in a food processor, cook the pasta, combine the two, and serve! Pesto comes from Genoa, on the Italian Riviera. Located between the mountains and the Mediterranean Sea, Genoa has a mild climate where herbs such as basil grow well.

Utensils

MIXING SPOON

HAND HELD
FOOD PROCESSOR

CHEESE
GRATER

COLANDER

1 Place a big pot of cold water on the stove over high heat. Separate the basil leaves from the stems. Place the leaves in a colander and rinse. Drain well and dry on a clean cloth.

2 Grate the cheeses. If you have one, use a grater with the little catcher underneath so that it is easier to gather up the grated cheese.

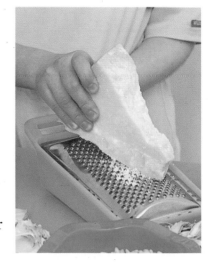

Ingredients

2 tablespoons (30 ml) toasted pine nuts

40 fresh basil leaves

12 oz (350 g) linguine pasta

2 tablespoons (30 ml) coarse salt to cook the pasta

⅔ cup (150 ml) extra-virgin olive oil

1 clove garlic

2 tablespoons (30 ml) each Parmesan and pecorino cheese

3 Place the basil, cheeses, pine nuts, garlic, oil, and salt in a bowl and chop with a hand held processor. If you have a food processor, place the ingredients in the bowl and chop and blend until the sauce is creamy.

4 When the water in the large pot is boiling, add the coarse salt and then the pasta. Cook for the amount of time shown on the package, about 10-12 minutes. Take 2 tablespoonfuls (30 ml) of the water from the pot and place in a serving dish. Drain the pasta in the colander and transfer it to the serving dish. Pour the basil sauce over the top and toss well. Serve immediately.

Gnocchi al ragù

Potato gnocchi with meat sauce

These little potato dumplings are a favorite dish all over Italy. The "gn" in *gnocchi* has the same pronunciation as the word "gnome," while the "ch" is pronounced like a "k." *Gnocchi* originally came from Verona, in northern Italy, where they were served with melted butter, sugar, and cinnamon. In Tuscany, they are called *topini*, which means "little mice."

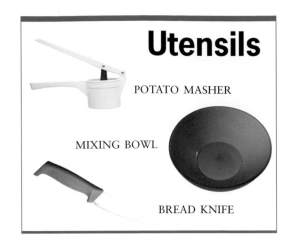

Utensils

POTATO MASHER

MIXING BOWL

BREAD KNIFE

1 Cook the unpeeled potatoes in a large pot of boiling water. Drain and set aside. When cool, remove the skins using your fingers, then mash.

2 Dust your hands with flour and begin working the flour and salt into the potatoes. Continue until the mixture is smooth and well mixed, but still soft.

Ingredients

2 lb (1 kg) boiling potatoes

3 cups (750 ml) all-purpose (plain) flour

dash of salt

13 oz (400 g) jar of already made Italian meat sauce

4 tablespoons (60 ml) grated Parmesan cheese

3 Take a handful of the mixture and roll it out into a long, thin "sausage" on a floured work surface. Cut the sausage into lengths about 1 inch (2–3 cm) long. Place a big pot full of cold water on the stove over high heat.

4 Pick up each *gnocchi* dumpling in one hand and run the tines of a fork along the edges so that it has lines running around it. If this is too difficult or takes too long, leave this step out. The *gnocchi* will still taste great!

5 Place the *gnocchi* on a lightly floured cloth. When the water is boiling, add a first batch of about 30 *gnocchi*. When they float up to the top, they are cooked. Scoop them out with a slotted spoon, and transfer them to a serving dish. Repeat until all the *gnocchi* are cooked. Heat the meat sauce and pour over the *gnocchi*. Sprinkle with the Parmesan and serve.

TIPS & TRICKS

To avoid being splashed by boiling water, place the gnocchi on a small, lightly floured dish, dip the edge into the water, and let them slip gently into the pot.

Carnevale

Carnevale, called "carnival" in English, is a time of merrymaking celebrated in many **Roman Catholic** countries before Lent. In Italy, the most important celebrations are held in the week leading up to Shrove Tuesday, the day before Ash Wednesday, and the start of the 40 days of Lent. To host an Italian *Carnevale* party, prepare the *cenci*, a Tuscan name for these traditional treats prepared all over Italy. Encourage your friends to dress up. Make papier-mâché masks and paint them in bright colors. It is traditional in Italy to throw **confetti**, set off fire crackers, and spray people with shaving cream! The best day to have your party is Shrove Tuesday.

This mask is one of many worn at carnival time in Venice.

Cenci

- 2 cups (500 ml) all-purpose (plain) flour
- 2 tablespoons (30 ml) butter, softened
- 2 eggs
- ¼ cup (60 ml) sugar
- dash of salt
- 2 tablespoons (30 ml) grated orange zest
- 1 cup (250 ml) olive oil for frying
- 4 tablespoons (60 ml) icing sugar

Sift the flour into a bowl and add the butter, eggs, sugar, salt, and orange zest. Stir with a wooden spoon, then knead with your hands until the dough is smooth and elastic. Cover with a clean cloth and leave for 30 minutes. Roll out into a thin sheet and cut into rectangular strips. Tie some into loose knots. Heat the oil in a deep skillet or frying pan and fry the cenci a few at a time until they are golden brown. Ask an adult to help you. Remove them with a slotted spoon and drain on paper towels. Sprinkle with icing sugar and serve at once.

When it comes to costumes, anything goes at Carnevale! In the past, people took advantage of wearing masks to poke fun at their rulers without fear of being recognized or punished for it.

These people are celebrating Carnevale in Piazza San Marco in the northern Italian city of Venice. Carnevale has become so famous that people from all over the world come to Venice to take part.

Traditionally, boys wore brightly colored Harlequin costumes, such as this one, at left. Harlequin, Arlecchino in Italian, was a well known comic character in Italian theater in the 16th and 17th centuries. Girls often dressed up as fairies. Today, both boys and girls wear costumes based on the their favorite movies or TV shows.

Risotto

Parmesan and saffron risotto

Rice was introduced to Western Europe by **Arab** invaders during the **Middle Ages.** Risotto was invented in the northern Italian city of Milan, where it is still a classic rice dish. This is a very good way to prepare rice because it cooks slowly, absorbing the flavors of all the other ingredients. **Saffron** adds a touch of color, turning the rice red or gold, depending on how much you add.

1 Chop the onion coarsely using a half-moon chopper or knife. In a deep-bottomed saucepan, **sauté** the onion in half the butter until it is golden.

TIPS & TRICKS

Keep the saucepan with the hot stock on the stove next to the risotto. This will keep it warm and make it easier and safer for you to add as the rice cooks.

Ingredients

1 medium red onion

6 tablespoons (90 ml) butter

2 cups (500 ml) rice (preferably Italian Arborio rice)

Italians traditionally cook risotto with wine. Use chicken stock instead.

4¼ cups (1 liter) chicken stock, made with boiling water and 1 stock cube

1 packet saffron

6 tablespoons (90 ml) grated Parmesan cheese

2 Add the rice to the saucepan and stir continuously over medium heat for about 2 minutes. Hold the saucepan firmly by the handle while stirring. The rice should swell and be lightly toasted.

Utensils

HALF-MOON CHOPPER

LADLE

CHEESE GRATER

CUTTING BOARD

WOODEN SPOON

DEEP-BOTTOMED SAUCEPAN

3 Dissolve the chicken stock cube in the hot water. Begin adding the stock to the rice a ladleful at a time, stirring as it is absorbed by the rice. Repeat until all of the stock has been absorbed.

4 Continue cooking and gradually adding more stock for about 20 minutes. Stir all the time so that the rice does not stick to the pan. Taste the rice after about 15 minutes to see if it is cooked. It should be soft, but firm or "*al dente,*" which means "firm to the bite."

5 When the rice is cooked, remove it from the heat and stir in the remaining butter.

6 Add the saffron and stir well so that the rice is evenly colored. Finally, stir in the Parmesan and serve.

Polpette al pomodoro

Meatballs with tomato sauce

These meatballs are bound to become one of your favorite dishes. The bread swells during cooking, making them soft as well as tasty. You can easily cut them with a fork and finish them in no time. The mixture is also fun to make because you can do it all with your hands. Who could resist squeezing the soft ground meat together with the other ingredients and rolling it into balls?

2 Grate the cheese and bread together into a large bowl. Keep your fingertips away from the grater.

1 Combine the tomatoes, salt, and oil in a deep saucepan. Cook over low heat for about 15 minutes, stirring often.

Utensils

GRATER

DEEP SKILLET
(FRYING PAN)

3 Combine the ground meat with the bread, cheese, eggs, salt, and pepper in a large mixing bowl. Mix well with your hands. Add a ladleful of the tomato sauce and stir it in with a spoon. Let the mixture cool.

Ingredients

6 cups (1.5 liters) tomato purée

salt to taste

¼ cup (60 ml) extra-virgin olive oil

1 lb (450 g) ground lean beef

1 loaf crusty white bread

3 eggs

2 cups (500 ml) grated Parmesan cheese

black pepper to taste

4 Rinse your hands in cold water to stop the mixture from sticking to them. Use your hands to form the mixture into smooth round balls each about the size of a large plum. Repeat this step until you have used up all the mixture. Place the meatballs on a plate.

5 Add the meatballs carefully to the tomato sauce, one at a time. Cook them in the sauce over low heat for 20–30 minutes without stirring. Shake the pan very gently from time to time. Serve the meatballs with the sauce spooned over top of them.

TIPS & TRICKS

Add the meatballs to the sauce very gently so that they don't break up. A good way to do this is to dip a tablespoon into cold water and scoop up a meatball. Dip it into the sauce, then pull the spoon out from under it.

Cotolette alla Milanese

Milanese-style veal scallops

This dish is also called Viennese **cutlets** or *Wiener schnitzel,* and some people think it was first made in Austria. Food historians in Italy have found letters that prove it was actually invented in Milan, over 1,000 years ago! These **veal** scallops are tasty and quick to make. You can serve them with French fries and a green salad for a complete family meal.

1 Break the eggs into a small bowl, add a dash of salt, and **beat** for 2–3 minutes with a fork.

2 Dry the veal scallops with paper towels. Then sprinkle lightly with salt on both sides.

TIPS & TRICKS

Boiling oil is very hot and can cause painful burns. Ask an adult to help you fry the scallops. If a little oil splashes from the pan onto your hands, run them under cold water. Try to buy scallops that have already been trimmed of fat. For vegetarians, use the same method to cook slices of eggplant.

Ingredients

2 eggs

dash of salt

6 veal scallops

1¾ cups (435 ml) dry bread crumbs

1 cup (250 ml) olive oil for frying

3 Dip the veal scallops one at a time into the bowl of egg. Make sure that every part of the veal is coated with egg. Let the extra egg drip back into the bowl as you lift the meat out.

4 Spread the bread crumbs out on a large plate. Lay each scallop in the bread crumbs and press down. Turn over and repeat. Shake off any extra bread crumbs.

Utensils

SLOTTED SPATULA

SKILLET (FRYING PAN)

5 Heat the oil in a large skillet and add the scallops one or two at a time. Make sure they do not overlap. Cook until a deep golden crust forms. Then turn over to cook the other side. Remove from the pan and drain on paper towels. Serve hot.

Pesce finto

False fish

This dish tastes good even if you don't normally like fish. The strong flavor of the fish is softened a little by the potatoes and mayonnaise. It is also fun to make because you can model the "fish" mixture with your hands, sculpting it into the shape of a fish. Decorate your fish with the mayonnaise, adding the mouth, gills, scales, and tail.

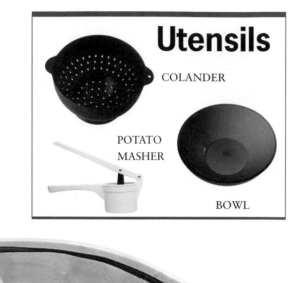

Utensils

COLANDER

POTATO MASHER

BOWL

1 Boil the potatoes in a pot of salted water for about 25 minutes or until tender. Drain in a colander. When they have cooled a little, peel off the skins with your fingers.

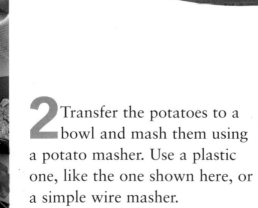

2 Transfer the potatoes to a bowl and mash them using a potato masher. Use a plastic one, like the one shown here, or a simple wire masher.

Ingredients

1½ lb (750 g) boiled potatoes

2 tablespoons (30 ml) finely chopped parsley

¾ cup (200 ml) canned tuna, squashed with a fork

½ cup (125 ml) mayonnaise, in a tube

dash of salt

1 clove garlic, finely chopped

3 Add the tuna, garlic, and parsley to the bowl with the potatoes. Mix well. Season with salt to taste.

4 Turn the mixture out on a large serving dish. You can use your hands to sculpt the mixture into the shape of a fish.

TIPS & TRICKS

Ask an adult to help move the pot of boiling water when draining potatoes. Always keep the mayonnaise in the refrigerator, especially just before you use it. Cold mayonnaise is easier to draw with.

5 Decorate the fish with the mayonnaise, squirting it out of the tube. Be creative by using a little parsley to add the fish's eye. You can draw in the gills, fins, and scales too.

Torta al cioccolato

Chocolate cake

If you get cravings for chocolate, this is the perfect recipe for you! When eaten in moderate quantities chocolate is not bad for you. It is not even true that it will give you pimples. The latest research shows that chocolate is a mood enhancer, which means that it makes you feel good. So do not feel guilty about loving this cake.

1 Place a large saucepan of water over medium heat. Put the chocolate and butter in a smaller pan and place it in the larger one. Cook, stirring all the time, until they have melted.

Ingredients

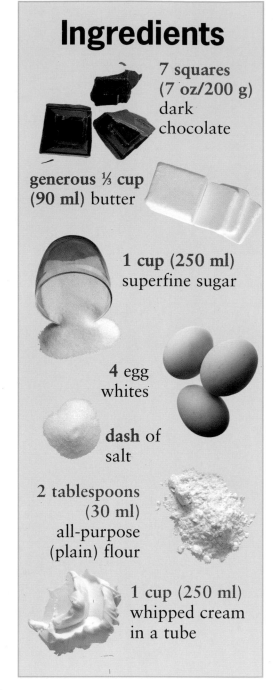

7 squares (7 oz/200 g) dark chocolate

generous ⅓ cup (90 ml) butter

1 cup (250 ml) superfine sugar

4 egg whites

dash of salt

2 tablespoons (30 ml) all-purpose (plain) flour

1 cup (250 ml) whipped cream in a tube

TIPS & TRICKS

Place the cake in the oven on the middle rack. Don't open the door during the first 20 minutes of cooking time, or your cake may go flat. Ask an adult to take the cake out of the oven or use thick oven mitts to protect your hands.

2 Remove the saucepan from the heat. Add the sugar and stir until it has **dissolved.** Gradually add the flour, stirring until well mixed. Set aside to cool.

33

3 **Separate** the eggs and beat the egg whites until stiff using a hand beater or an electric mixer. Add salt first so the eggs will be ready sooner.

4 When the chocolate mixture is **lukewarm,** carefully mix in the egg whites. Use a spatula to lift up the chocolate mixture and gently blend in the egg whites.

5 **Grease** and flour a 10-inch (24 cm) diameter springform pan and pour the mixture into it. Bake in a preheated oven at 300°F (150°C) for about 25 minutes. The cake should have a light crust but still be soft inside. To test if the cake is cooked, poke a toothpick into the middle; if it comes out clean the cake is ready. Remove from the oven and turn out onto a wire rack to cool.

6 When the cake is cool, decorate it with the whipped cream.

Tiramisù

Creamy chocolate surprise

This dessert is so good that four different Italian regions – Lombardy, Emilia-Romagna, Veneto, and Tuscany – all claim to have invented it! It is fun to make and tasty to eat. When you serve it, your friends and family will think you are a gourmet chef. The name of this dessert is pronounced with the accent on the last syllable and means "pick me up."

TIPS & TRICKS

*If your local supermarket or Italian food store does not have mascarpone cheese, use the same quantity of cream cheese in its place. This dessert needs to be **chilled** at least two hours in the refrigerator, so remember to start early. If you do not like the taste of coffee, replace it with the same quantity of raspberry syrup.*

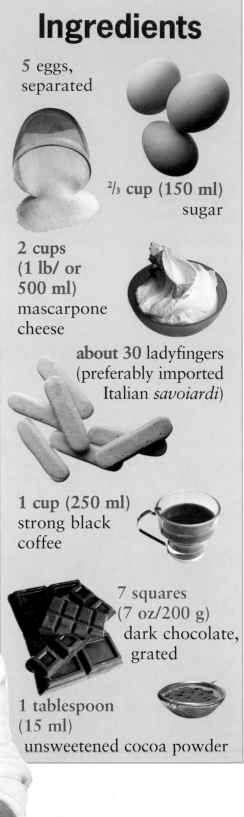

Ingredients

5 eggs, separated

²/₃ cup (150 ml) sugar

2 cups (1 lb/ or 500 ml) mascarpone cheese

about 30 ladyfingers (preferably imported Italian *savoiardi*)

1 cup (250 ml) strong black coffee

7 squares (7 oz/200 g) dark chocolate, grated

1 tablespoon (15 ml) unsweetened cocoa powder

Utensils

EGG BEATER

MIXING BOWL

SPATULA

5 Put the cocoa in a sifter and sift evenly over the top to finish. Place in the refrigerator for at least two hours before serving.

1 Separate the eggs and use the spatula to beat the yolks and sugar until they are creamy and light in color. Stir in the mascarpone a bit at a time and mix well.

2 Beat the egg whites until they form a stiff mixture. Carefully stir the beaten egg whites into the egg yolks and mascarpone until well mixed.

Stir the egg whites into the yolks carefully so that the mixture stays light and fluffy.

Dip the **ladyfingers** *quickly into the coffee so that they absorb a little, but do not become too soggy.*

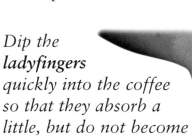

3 Cover the bottom of a serving dish with a layer of the mixture. Dip some ladyfingers into the coffee and then place them in a layer over the cream.

Use the spatula to spread the cream over the ladyfingers in an even layer.

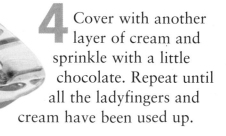

4 Cover with another layer of cream and sprinkle with a little chocolate. Repeat until all the ladyfingers and cream have been used up.

Gelato di crema con salsa al cioccolato

Ice cream with chocolate sauce

36

Ice cream with hot chocolate sauce is one of the most delicious ways to finish a meal. Some believe ice cream was invented in China, around 3,000 B.C. The ancient Chinese mixed snow with fruit and honey and, in time, ice cream became popular all over the world. Italian pastry chefs perfected the art of making ice cream in the 1500s and called it *gelato*.

TIPS & TRICKS

If you do not have an ice cream maker, place the mixture in a freezer proof bowl and place in the freezer. After two hours, stir quickly and put it back in the freezer. Repeat twice.

1 Separate the eggs. In a mixing bowl, beat the egg yolks and the sugar with a **whisk** until they are pale and creamy.

Utensils

WHISK

MIXING SPOON

SMALL SAUCEPAN

SAUCEPAN

ICE CREAM MAKER

Ingredients

4 egg yolks

½ cup (125 ml) sugar

1 cup (250 ml) milk

¾ cup (200 ml) cream

8 squares (8 oz/250 g) dark chocolate

2 tablespoons (30 ml) butter

2 Add the milk and then half the cream gradually to the mixture, beating all the time until they have been completely absorbed.

3 Pour the mixture into the ice cream maker and follow the instructions to make the ice cream. If you do not have an ice cream maker see the Tips & Tricks box for instructions on how to make ice cream by hand.

4 When the ice cream is ready, place the chocolate, butter, and remaining cream in a small saucepan. Fill a larger saucepan half full of water and put the smaller one inside. Place over medium heat until the ingredients have all melted together. Put the ice cream in a serving bowl and pour the chocolate sauce over top.

Glossary

anchovies small fish, often salted and dried.

appetizer a small amount of a food or drink served at the beginning of a meal.

Arabs A native or inhabitant of Arabia, an area located between the Red Sea and the Persian Gulf.

baguette baked bread formed in the shape of a long rectangle.

beat to mix a liquid or soft paste rapidly.

capers unopened buds of a flower grown in the Mediterranean regions and often preserved in brine or salt

chill to refrigerate, but not to freeze.

chop to cut into tiny, fine pieces using a knife or food processor.

coarsely chopped to cut in larger pieces, not in a fine, smooth texture.

confetti small pieces of paper, thrown in the air at festive events.

cutlets a flat ball of finely chopped food, such as fish, or vegetables.

drizzle to let something fall in fine drops or a fine stream.

dice to cut food into tiny cubes using a knife.

dissolve when one thing disintegrates into another, making a solution.

grease to coat a pan with oil or melted butter.

grate to cut foods into small, thin pieces by rubbing them against a grater.

knead the act of mixing and pressing dough by hand before it is baked.

ladyfingers sweet, sponge cakes known in Italy as "savoiardi."

lukewarm something that is moderately warm.

Middle Ages the period in European history during the late 5th century to the 1400s.

mix to combine ingredients in a bowl.

pasta noodle-like pastes or doughs, such as spaghetti.

pinch a measurement amount held in the tips of two fingers.

rise when dough swells or puffs up from the action of yeast.

Roman Catholic a member of the Christian church led by the Pope.

saffron the orange stigma of a crocus flower used for coloring and flavoring food.

sauté to fry food lightly over medium heat in oil.

separate in cooking, to divide an egg's yoke from its white, both to be used at different stages of a recipe

serrated having a grooved edge.

sift to separate the fine and the coarse parts of flour with a sifter.

skillet a small long-handled saucepan, or frying pan.

sprinkle to scatter in separate drops.

toss to throw lightly without force, within the dish or bowl.

veal the meat of a calf, used for food.

whisk a utensil used to whip food.

Index